SEARCHING FOR TAO CANYON

Searching For
TAO
CANYON

Text by Jeremy Schmidt
Photos by Pat Morrow,
Jeremy Schmidt,
and Art Twomey

RMB

I have not tired of the wilderness; rather I enjoy its beauty and the vagrant life I lead, more keenly all the time. I prefer the saddle to the streetcar and star-sprinkled sky to a roof, the obscure and difficult trail, leading into the unknown, to any paved highway, and the deep peace of the wild to the discontent bred by cities.... It is enough that I am surrounded by beauty.

—Everett Ruess

Previous page: Some slots you can walk or scramble into; others are accessible only by playing spider games.

Right: Art Twomey adjusts his Graflex Speed Graphic 4x5 camera.

ART TWOMEY

He was the original fun hog. "Think about it," he would say, "how little time most people spend doing what they really want to do." He called it fun hogging, as in getting as much fun as you could cram into whatever time was available. To some, that would seem inadequate as a life philosophy — to devote yourself to having fun. But Art was speaking of much more than simple fun. He meant passions, values and authentic desires — the things that turn enjoyment into purpose. He meant it on two levels: do things you want to do, and do them because they are worth doing, because they make you feel good about yourself, your community, your world. Art built a career out of doing what made him happy, and it was all to the good. His passions mattered. Glaciologist, geologist, environmental activist (he was the main proponent of the Purcell Wilderness Conservancy, the largest of its kind in British Columbia), film-maker, photographer, ski guide, mountaineer, mule skinner and mentor. We dedicate this book to him.

Pat Morrow
Jeremy Schmidt

Immediately below the rim, where the sky is no longer visible, the light is a warm gold. Farther down it becomes red, then purple, then deep blue, and then – only if the slot is deep enough – black: a rainbow of colour in a cool, silent, rounded room.

CONTENTS

HEADS UP, FELLOW DESERT RATS

This is not a guide book.

We're not going to tell you names or give directions to these exquisitely fragile places. It might be foolish to think we can help protect them by obscuring locations and calling them by our own unofficial names. But the idea has its roots in the photo to the right.

More than 40 years ago, Art Twomey published it in the Sierra Club's annual nature calendar. He called the place by its real name, and quickly regretted it.

Mail poured in, people asking where this was. How could this be rock? How could it be a canyon, this lighthearted, almost aerial thing possessing movement, wind, flowing water and trickster light? Hundreds wanted to go there to see it for themselves.

Art understood the risk of telling people. He knew how easily the rock could be damaged even by a careful person. He took to answering, "I found it, so can you." He might have added that Tao, the name we attached to our conceptual ideal of a slot canyon, means simply "The Way" in its original Chinese use.

It was Art who introduced us to slot canyons. With him and other friends, for about ten years beginning in 1975, we found many good ones and made the photographs in this book — all of them on film, mostly Kodachrome 25, not a digital one in the bunch.

Since then, some of these places have become famous, instagrammed nearly to death and no doubt recognizable to slot canyon cognoscenti. Nonetheless, we are sticking to Art's old policy of not naming and not giving directions. It was a good policy then, and it still is.

Art's 4x5 transparency, Sandstone Alcove, published in the 1974 Sierra Club Wilderness Calendar.

May your rivers
flow without
end ... down into a
desert of red rock,
blue mesas, domes and
pinnacles and grottos
of endless stone,
and down again into
a deep vast ancient
unknown chasm where
bars of sunlight blaze
on profiled cliffs ...
where something
strange and more
beautiful and more full
of wonder than your
deepest dreams waits
for you – beyond that
next turning of the
canyon walls.

—Edward Abbey,
Desert Solitaire

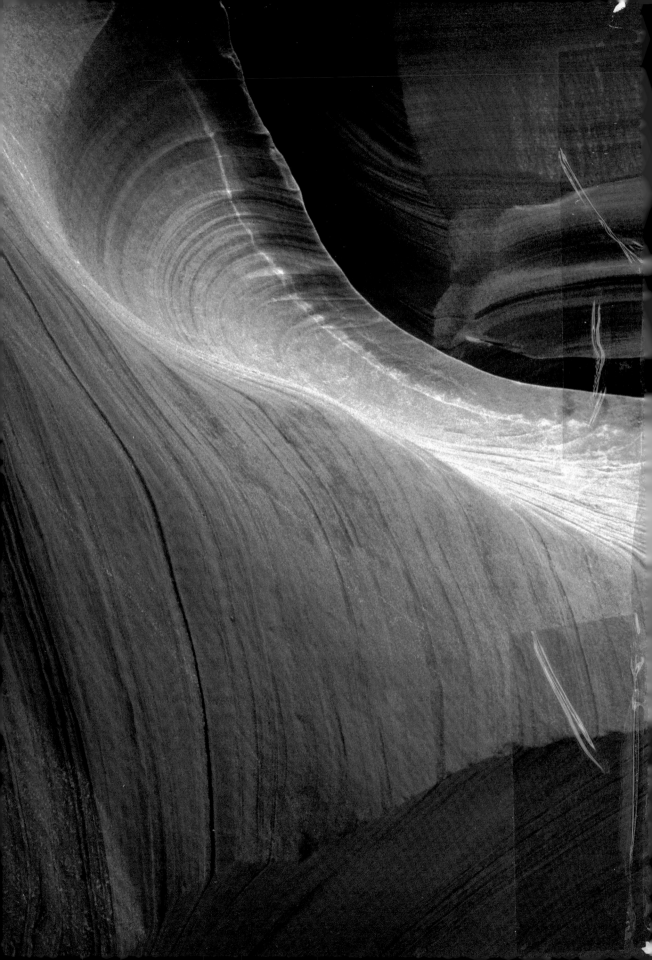

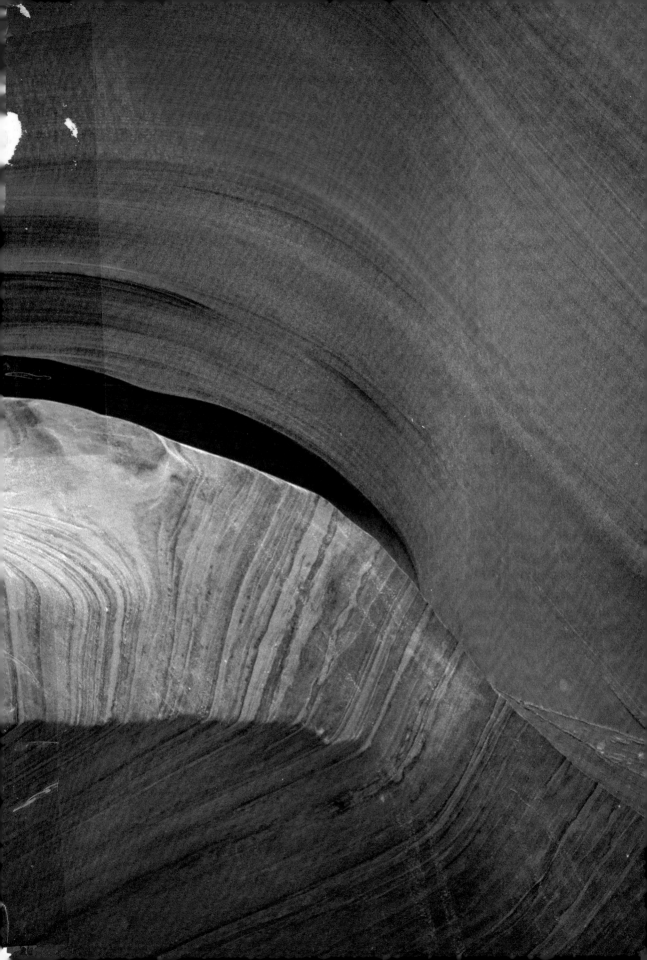

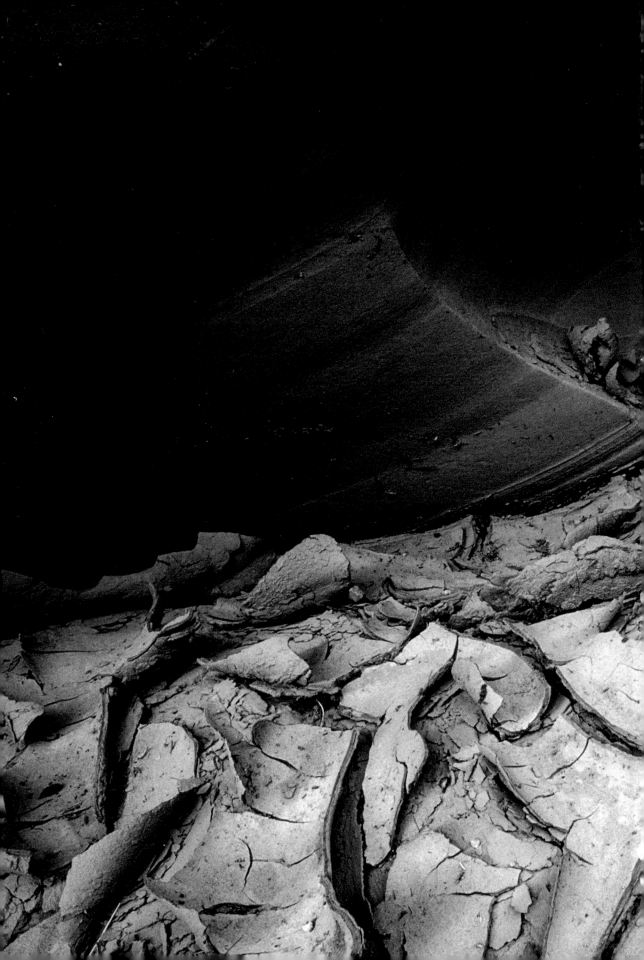

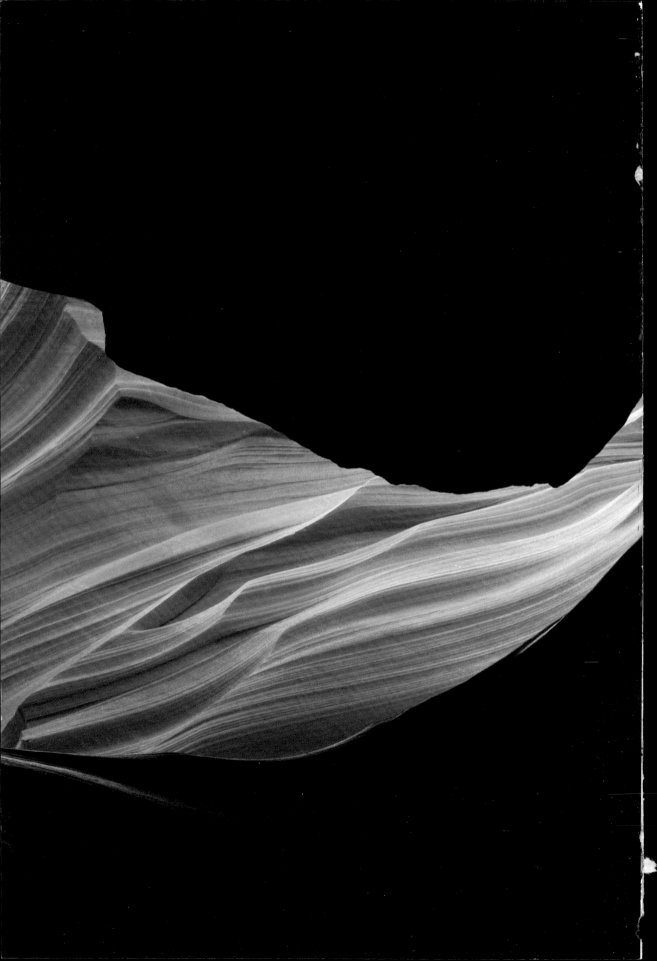

In the
JAW
of the
DRAGON

In April 1970, Art Twomey set out across the northern Arizona desert with his friend Joanna Coleman. They carried heavy packs loaded with camping gear, a large-format camera and food for a week.

It was a hot day. The walking was hard. Blackbrush scratched their legs. Sand rolled under their feet. The desert seemed to stretch ahead unbroken, a featureless plain all the way to the blue mass of Navajo Mountain, some 50 miles away. But they knew, because they had been in this country before, that canyons filled that seemingly empty space. Hundreds of canyons large and small, drawn like the fretwork on a maple leaf, dissected the smooth bedrock into a maze of sandstone domes, pinnacles, arches, overhanging alcoves and shadowed, echoing, hidden spaces. You couldn't see them from a distance. You had to get close, by walking.

They had a particular canyon in mind, a branch of a branch of a canyon that joined the Colorado River in Glen Canyon. Or rather, it once

We called it Super Groove. Several miles long, it ended high in the wall of a much larger canyon and gave life to a spectacular waterfall during flash floods.

did, before the Glen Canyon Dam stopped the river and turned it into the motorboat playground called Lake Powell. Before the dam, when the river was alive, anyone could float the canyon. You could float almost any little craft. Rowboat. Canoe. Inner tube. It was that easy, a welcoming warm-water trip through a heartbreakingly beautiful place. You would drift past dozens of side-canyons, maybe hundreds, every one of them waiting for you to stop, to explore, to see what lay hidden in their sculptured passages. You wouldn't have to walk across rugged desert to get into them. You could simply wander upstream from the Colorado wearing nothing more than tennis shoes and shorts, or not even that, and revel in the splendour of those places.

That ended after the dam, not yet even completed, closed a steel gate in 1963 and the lake began to rise. You need a motorboat now, to see what's left of the great canyon. Art disliked motorboats. He and Joanna could have paddled a canoe on the lake, but that meant bucking the wakes of water skiers all the long way from the marina to the flooded mouth of their intended canyon. They preferred walking in from above, across the open desert.

Art had found the canyon on a topographic map. It appeared as a series of squiggly brown contour lines crowded against a blue line indicating water. That meant cliffs and a stream. As for anything more, a paper map could only hint at the true nature of the place. It might or might not be what they hoped to find. Their hopes were vivid. They anticipated water flowing clear and improbably cold over slickrock ledges and red sand beneath high arcing walls. There would be shade alternating with hot sun, and little waterfalls, and pools for swimming. Cottonwood trees would be rattling new leaves in gentle breezes. They expected frogs croaking, hummingbirds

nesting, canyon wrens singing, sego lilies and prickly pear blooming — a rich reward for a few miles of hard walking.

Their hike started out as they expected, sand and thorny shrubs and not much else. But canyon country delights in dealing surprises. Just when you think you

Loaded for slots. Art tramps across the desert with a full pack, including rock-climbing gear, tripod, cameras, food, camping equipment and whatever else he might need for a week in the canyons.

know where you're going, and how to get there, you find you don't know much at all. True to form, a few miles from their planned destination, as if enjoying its big joke, the desert opened in a jack-o-lantern grin. They came upon it suddenly — a ragged crevasse in glaring bedrock, a dark slash directly across their path of travel. It was almost narrow enough to leap across, if they'd been brave enough, but it made them nervous just to stand on the edge of what seemed a bottomless void.

What a strange canyon. How deep? What was down there? Art tossed a stone. It ricocheted into the dark, sending back a series of echoing reports, rock hitting rock. Then silence. No telling how far it had fallen.

They started walking, looking for a place to get across, following the canyon upstream. In places, the rim resembled a giant funnel, its smooth walls sloping down 40 or 50 feet to a narrow mouth, and then — blackness. If you slipped it would swallow you, no stopping the slide. In other places, the canyon rims were six or eight feet apart, like balconies on opposite sides of a narrow street. A dark narrow street with no apparent bottom.

At those places, they would lean out precariously, peering downward, but the contrast between the sun-hammered rimrock and the shadows within was too great for them to see what was below. More stones were dropped; the same distorted reports of clattering rock came back.

After half a mile of walking, they came to the end. Or rather, the beginning, a place where the canyon was no more than a shallow ravine. Had they encountered it at this point, they might have crossed it without a thought and kept on walking. Instead, they dropped their packs and slipped down into the shadows.

One of our favourite canyons was pristine when we first saw it. Several years later, someone had chiselled steps into the smooth fluted surface.

The softest stuff
in the world
Penetrates quickly
the hardest;
Insubstantial, it enters
Where no room is.
—Laozi
(trans. Raymond
B. Blakney)

At this point, the floor of the ravine was a smooth slick-rock slab, in the middle of which ran a tiny waterworn groove. Quickly it grew to something more. It became a narrow slit, hardly a foot across, diving steeply underground. Water had carved it. The water had pulsed through in flash floods. Finding a weakness in the bedrock, it had sliced downward like a wire melting through butter, except that as it went, it twisted on itself, writhing, coiling, hesitating, then plunging deeper, hurrying toward the distant Colorado River.

Dry now, the canyon looked like the sort of place only a snake with wings would have any reason to venture into. Nonetheless, drawn by curiosity, turning their shoulders sideways, Art and Joanna edged their way deep into the bedrock.

What they found was an illusory landscape that twisted their perceptions and tweaked their sense of reality. It was a desert funhouse, a whimsical structure of cool, shady rooms connected by narrow passages, beautifully rounded and lit from above. The light bounced down in the same way their tossed pebbles had done, ricocheting, echoing, becoming distorted and, the farther they walked, becoming almost too dim to see by. Almost never was the sky visible.

The shapes were extraordinary. Water had carved the sandstone in its own form, complete with waves and eddies. It was liquid made solid. Motion petrified.

It made no visual sense yet compelled the senses.

Art climbed out to fetch his Graflex Speed Graphic 4x5 camera, squeezed back down to a small jug-shaped room where he could set up a tripod, and exposed several sheets of Ektachrome film. That done, he and Joanna set off again for their original destination, which turned out to be just what they had hoped for.

Not until he got home, processed the film and saw the

photographs did Art realize how unusual a place they had found. There was light down there that he hadn't seen, or rather hadn't interpreted. It was a gentle, multicoloured light that mixed with the fluted sandstone in a way that defied ordinary perception but revealed itself on film. The pictures showed a dizzy confusion of up and down, in and out, conveying no sense of scale or substance. The pictures were at least as weird as the place itself.

The best of those photos, which he called Sandstone Alcove, appeared on the cover of the 1974 Sierra Club Wilderness Calendar. At that time the calendar was a premier publishing venue for the sort of photography Art practised — large-format natural landscapes. It was perhaps the first slot photograph to appear in a widely distributed, popular publication. It tantalized thousands of viewers who had never seen any landscape to compare with it, and caused a minor stir. Hundreds of people wrote the publishers wanting to know where the photo had been made. One man wrote a long poem. Some accused Art of manipulation, as if he had used lights and distorting lenses. These days, with computer-enhanced images all around us, people might dismiss Sandstone Alcove as a work of imagination.

But of course it existed, in solid rock and ever-changing light, a fantastic space both physical and ethereal with its own definition of how three physical dimensions can seem to represent more.

I knew Art from college in the Midwest. We both studied natural science — geology for him, zoology for me. But it was the outdoors that defined us and motivated us, and in the end we both realized that academic careers were a poor fit for people who wanted more than anything to free-range the world's wild places.

In 1975, Art was living in British Columbia, where he had built a cabin 24 miles from the nearest town and nine miles from the nearest plowed road. From that splendid but remote location, he was pursuing a career as a film-maker and nature photographer. I was living in Yellowstone National Park at Old Faithful, working as a winterkeeper. My job was simple: to keep the roofs from collapsing under the weight of snow. That meant shovelling them from time to time. The work was easy, and honest, and as clean as work can be. Pay was almost nothing, but there was nothing to spend money on, and most of the time there wasn't much work to do. So I was pleased when Art called to ask if he could come stay for a while. A Canadian television program had hired him to make a film on Yellowstone in winter.

He arrived in February with a friend, also from British Columbia — Pat Morrow — a photographer and climber who shared our passion for wild places.

They spent a month. We skied, cooked Mexican food, drank home brew, stood in the moonlight among the geysers and worked our cameras. The snow was deep that winter. Overnight temperatures fell to minus 40 and lower. The geyser basin became a strange world lost in a fog of mist from the hot springs. Ice formed on everything. Geysers exploded with white violence when boiling water met subzero air. Bison and elk moved slowly, their coats white from gathered frost.

We revelled in winter, but in the evenings, talk turned to the southwest and Art's slot canyon pictures and the images we could make there. We looked at photos and maps, and decided that in the spring we would head that way together, to look for more canyons like the one where Art had found Sandstone Alcove.

Route finding with a tripod, Art follows the receding waters of a recent flash flood.

Art grew up in Tucson, Arizona. He counted among his influences an older friend, Tad Nichols. Tad was a sort of fun-hog mentor to high school—aged Art. A landscape photographer, Tad made frequent trips to canyon country, often with his friends, actress and activist Katie Lee and river guide Frank Wright. Among their favourite places was Glen

Canyon, where the sun-warmed Colorado River flowed gently through a wilderness of slickrock, sand beaches and exquisitely sculpted slot canyons.

Since there were no rapids to deal with, they could put any little floating craft on the river — canoes, military surplus life rafts, row boats, inner tubes — load them with

Three-dimensional topsy turvy. Jeremy and Art work different angles of the kaleidoscopic funhouse.

canned food and drift for weeks beneath walls reverberating with light and the sounds of the river moving. In his book of photographs from that time, *Glen Canyon: Images of a Lost World*, Tad wrote, "It's like standing in a great Cathedral. There's a spirituality in that. I can't describe it any other way."

It was a beloved place for the few who knew it, a place of beauty where time seemed to mean nothing.

Except that time meant everything. In 1963, the Bureau of Reclamation (a.k.a. "Wreck-the-nation") closed the gates on its new Glen Canyon Dam (a.k.a. the "Damn Dam"). Lake Powell began to fill with stilled water, covering, smothering, turning a place of unique beauty into a silt-shrouded graveyard, and letting loose a cascading plague of environmental damage downstream in the Grand Canyon. In the waning days before the waters rose and destroyed the places he loved, Tad bought a motorboat so he could move faster on the river, something that earlier he would have thought sacrilegious. But these were profane times, and he wanted to revisit the best places before they were lost. Cathedral in the Desert, Hidden Passage, Music Temple, Labyrinth Canyon, Forbidding Canyon and so many others. Tad went frequently, often alone. One of Art's biggest regrets was that he never accepted Tad's offer to go with him. "Tad told me to come," Art said. "He told me high school wasn't worth missing Glen Canyon. I thought I needed to keep my grades up — what a mistake."

By the time we three started poking around in slot canyons, Lake Powell was nearly full and covered with motorboats and water skiers. We knew we had missed out on the central splendour of the region. We felt sometimes that our explorations were scrounging trips, as if we were scavengers picking at the remaining scraps, until we realized that even among the scraps there were glittering treasures.

Into the sweet air and the smell of yellow pine, into the grasslands among the ancient cinder cones, into the freedom of the open range. Good God but it's a relief to escape, if only for an hour, the squalid anthills, big or little, Show Low or Shanghai of twentieth-century man. A world without open country would be a universal jail.

—Edward Abbey,
The Fool's Progress

For us, wandering through canyon country proved the counter-truths of fun hogging. It embodied the thrill of being unconstrained in God's own backyard and taught us the higher value of leaving nature the hell alone — the way it was made.

We were on the loose, with a whole continent to roam around in, much of it wild and beautiful and open to anyone with the desire to see what was out there — especially the young, for when you're young, so much is fresh and shiny new, and every discovery is something no one else knows about, and you hold the knowledge of Paradise like a personal jewel that you alone have discovered.

That first year, while snow still covered the mountains of British Columbia and Yellowstone, we met in red rock country and spent two months scouring the region for the narrowest, deepest, most visually alluring canyons we could find. We did it again in the fall, and then the following spring. It became an informal tradition — especially in spring, when, weary of severe northern winters and eager for the fragrance and soul-warming colours of desert sand, we would get together in the slickrock with new ideas and new maps, and poke our noses into the most obscure corners we could find.

Over a span of ten years or so, we shinnied and wiggled and swam and walked through many canyons, large and small, not all of them pleasant. Some were as lovely as that first one where Art shot Sandstone Alcove. Others were grim places filled with cold water and cold, dull light. We oozed through those, slipping and shivering, and didn't go back.

Finding slots could be a matter of dumb luck. They showed up unpredictably, almost always in massive, homogeneous sandstone, the pure stuff uncut by shale, mudstone or other messy layers. Michelangelo demanded perfect

Carrara marble. To the desert sculptor — nature, that is, wielding wind and water as its primary tools — Navajo sandstone is prime. Geologists have a beautiful word for this kind of stone: aeolian, from the Greek god Aeolus, Keeper of the Winds. Up to 2,200 feet thick, white or pink in colour, Navajo sandstone began as dunes piled high by Jurassic winds in a Sahara-like desert. Its neighbour the Entrada sandstone is good, and so is the Wingate, both of them deeply red and orange. But slots occur in all kinds of rock, and knowing the stratigraphy only begins to narrow things down.

Slot canyons can appear suddenly. Blink and you'll miss one of the best; it crosses under a major highway, clearly visible but barely noticeable at 65 miles an hour. We came across another while driving back roads northwest of the Colorado River, thinking we had left slot country behind. At first it seemed to be just another gully, one of 50 like it that we had crossed that day. But instead of a sandy bottom, it was rock, sliced down the middle by a 200-foot-deep slot. The road crew had built their bridge by pushing tree trunks and old cars into it until they formed a plug strong enough to hold gravel. They left plenty of room for the stream to flow under the junkyard plug, and solved their problem cheaply. Common-sense engineering.

Usually, finding a new slot involved a lot of walking, more or less blindly scouring the dendritic headwaters of major canyons where streams were small and intermittent, and slots were likely to begin. Maps might show a thin blue line, or not. Even on large-scale topographic maps, contour lines run across slots with scarcely a nick. You wouldn't know there was anything to see except flat desert, prickly pear and blackbrush tearing at your legs. Then the sand gives way to smooth rock, the rock slopes downhill slightly, and within a few steps you're standing on the edge of one. It

Previous pages:

A narrow passage darkly lit by the cold blue sky leads to an opening, warmly radiant in reflected sunlight.

This idyllic scene looks complete, but at the moment when we first arrived, we surprised a desert bighorn sheep that had been grazing on a ledge just out of the frame. The magnificent creature took one look at us and strode purposefully from sight.

runs across the surface like a pumpkin smile, grinning its inscrutable black riddle. Too dark to see beyond the screaming brilliance of the sunlit rim, and deep. Deeper than you can tell.

But it's narrow enough to jump across. You look for a place with a good landing on the other side, but when you

No place for a claustrophobe.

step back to make the leap, something about that hollow darkness — something in the darkness — wells up and nails you to the rock. Were it a mud puddle or hedge you would jump it with no hesitation, but here it's not so simple. There's something unknown and not nice about what lies below. Something unpredictable. Momentum should carry you across. Of course it will. But you're not sure you believe it.

A few slots put us off to the point that we haven't yet gone into them. Too deep, too dark. They had water in the bottoms, slimy water with evil, rotting stuff floating in it, slippery ledges dropping into them. Wallowing through those murky passages provided a kind of perverse pleasure for a while, until the novelty of being sewer rats wore off. It was hard to find beauty in places like that. They just led deeper into deeper gloom.

The narrow, usually dry slots were comforting, in their enclosed, enclosing way. They had the finest sculpting and the most abstract juxtapositions of curving shapes and shadow. They were enough in their own right, but if we followed them far enough, the best ones opened into much bigger canyons, still slots in their general shape but scaled up and big enough to hold churches. These were glorious. You wouldn't have to knock off the steeples to fit whole churches down there in the shade of opposing rims that nearly touched, but below them the canyons widened out to form vast echoing amphitheatres. It might have sounded good to hear a pipe organ in those spaces. It surely would have. Yet to us those big slot canyons were better than any churches could ever be, and the music that filled them was older even than the rocks.

Ankle deep in sweet-flowing streams, we craned our necks upward, 400 feet or more, to where swallows and swifts soared through the domes and belfries. The birds were electric beings. Against shadowed overhangs,

catching sunlight in their feathers, they lit up and sparkled with every wingbeat, bright flickerings against the dark rock. Then, sailing out to where the bright sky was their backdrop, as if switching off their lights, they went black. The rock behind — on. The sky behind — off. On, off, on, off, around they went in endless circuit, spiralling after one another in a distant, mysterious dance.

At every turn there was enchantment of the sort Loren Eiseley meant when he wrote, "If there is magic on this planet, it is contained in water." The canyons were water as much as they were rock. They were carved by water, were filled with the music of its flowing. Water sustained the birds that danced in the air above and the insects upon which they fed. It dampened the maidenhair fern and yellow columbines on dripping walls, and filled the pools where frogs made their own croaky but harmonious songs of water.

These big canyons could be as narrow as your shoulders at the bottom. They could be wide enough to hold hills of

Margie Jamieson demonstrates Celtic boulder-heaving techniques (above). Art rappelling (right).

Following pages: The surface barely hints at what lies hidden below.

sand covered with tall grass, cacti, shrub oak and desert wildflowers — good camping spots above the damp. Some openings held groves of old cottonwood trees loaded with birds overhead and lizards clattering in the dry leaves on the ground. At night, bats flashed across narrow strips of starlit sky. Coyotes, skunks, deer and the occasional mountain lion left tracks in the wet sand for us to find in the morning.

The moon, when it shone full, left us with nothing to do but gape, and bless our good fortune.

It was a different time in a little-known place. Moab, Utah — even Moab, now the noisy epicentre for canyon country recreation — was a dusty former uranium-mining town with a few local companies offering tours in beat-up Second World War surplus jeeps. Ed Abbey's signature book *Desert Solitaire* was quietly gaining popularity, but Abbey wasn't yet the enviro-icon he would become. There were no guidebooks or GPS units to show us the way and spoil

Above: Shovels were a simple, sometimes-effective substitute for four-wheel drive. Left: The perfect arcing parabola of our campsite was filled in the late evening with the whoo who-whoo of a great horned owl and in the predawn with shrills of swifts foraging in the sky.

the joy of discovery. No mountain bikes, dirt bikes, bungee jumping or ziplines. No helicopter tours, parasails, flying squirrel suits or personal aircraft, never the angry buzz of drones carrying cameras, no ATVs, and few vehicles overall. The explosion of outdoor toys that have so altered the wild landscape, and the way people get around in it, lay in the future like a hidden crate of dynamite at the end of an unlit fuse.

We felt free, and we were, and we had the canyons to ourselves. We rarely encountered anyone else in them and came to think of slot canyons as our personal secret gardens. We spent days, even weeks, in the best ones. With tripods set, we watched shadows move, and shapes shift as the sun arced through the unseen sky above. We hung from ropes, wedged ourselves into narrows hardly wide enough for a tennis shoe, or perched in little waterworn rooms high above the canyon floor, their walls carved round like the inside of a cured squash.

Every image we made was on film, mostly Kodachrome, ISO 25, no artificial light, tripods essential.

Art and Margie perform their slickrock version of Wayang, Indonesian shadow puppet theater.

Turnaround time to see the result of our processed slides was a minimum of one week. It took a couple of batches of film, and spreading out our slides on a borrowed light table at the tiny newspaper office in Page, Arizona, to see that we were initially way off in our approach to capturing the essence of these kaleidoscopic places. We learned a whole new way of seeing subterranean light and adjusted our photographic approach accordingly.

Long exposures, usually 15 to 30 seconds, brought out colours that were hard to see with the naked eye. Some colours were modified by the way film reacted to different wavelengths during long exposures, an effect called reciprocity failure. Yet we enhanced nothing. All the colours were there, in the actual spectrum of the slots. We learned to see the different tones, and to anticipate how they would look on film, and then to wait for changes in ambient light (we tried to avoid harsh direct light) that would bring the results we hoped for. It made for a lot of time sitting still, studying shadows and watching the drifting harmonics of indirect, reverberated sunlight. Stretches of canyon that casual visitors breeze through in mere minutes today would hold us captive all day long.

In 1975, Canyonlands National Park was only 11 years old. Arches was younger yet. The Park Service was just trying to learn what was out there, and how they should manage it. The Bureau of Land Management (BLM) owned much of what lay between the marquee attractions, and the BLM was interested mainly in stuff like cows and uranium prospecting, not the occasional young folks with backpacks and thrift-store clothing. The BLM didn't care what we did.

Neither did the Navajo, as far as we could tell. The reservation, most of it in northern Arizona, is a huge and spectacular landscape that drew us like a magnet. Roads there, even major highways, weren't fenced; we could turn

> I don't care two hoots about civilization. I want to wander in the wild.
> —Jane Goodall

off practically anywhere and follow rough two-track paths made by pickup trucks. There wasn't yet a formal permit system for visitors, something the Navajo rightly put in place once they saw the combined threat of environmental damage and invasion of privacy brought on by industrial recreation. For us, although we knew we were on private land, permission was a matter of driving where the tracks took us. If we found a promising canyon we wanted to go into, we learned to look for the nearest dwelling, drop off a load of firewood that we'd gathered as we drove and have a chat before going farther. Like people everywhere, the folks we met wanted to know who was poking around in their backyards. But they were almost always friendly and welcoming about it, and curious. You want to go down there? Sure, but why would you do that?

Pat and I climbed out of a slot one day to find that a

Navajo kids were entertained by our wanting to go down into the cave-like cracks but didn't want to join us when we offered to help them see what we saw.

Navajo family had arrived while we were below the rim. They were putting up a fence around their dry farm corn patch — hard work chiselling postholes into solid sandstone with a heavy, sharpened steel bar as a drilling tool. The cornfield, a two-acre Sahara of loose sand, seemed a hopeless endeavour, and yet the Navajos — two grandparents, five adults and a scattering of children — spoke cheerfully of the water deep under the sand that the roots would find. The corn would grow, they said, if only they could get the fence up and keep the cows out.

After a few minutes of gardening talk, someone inquired politely about what we were doing out here down in that dark slot. Taking pictures? One of the younger women translated for the older couple, who laughed and shook their heads.

It was a crazy thing to do. None of them had ever been into a slot, although their home stood half a mile from the edge of this one. Why, they wanted to know, did we go into those places? Pat went to the van and returned with prints of pictures we had taken earlier, thinking they would explain the attraction. The Navajos passed them around and returned them, unimpressed. It was still a crazy thing to do.

We asked, "Are there any others like this one around here?"

"There's one about a mile that way," the young woman said, pointing with her lips, Navajo style, "but you can get around it. It isn't a bad one."

In books about canyon country we found chilling tales. A Navajo ancestral legend relates the epic journey of the Twin Brothers on their search for their father. Changing Woman, their mother, sends them off with advice and warnings. Beware, she says, of the crushing-rock canyon, a grim narrows that closes suddenly, like great jaws, upon travellers. She provides prayers and incantations, and tells them the name by which they must address the canyon to prevent it from crushing them. In case that fails, she gives them magic feathers as a last resort. And so it happens. They arrive in the canyon. The walls begin to close. The boys are petrified with fear. They cannot speak the canyon's name or say the prayers, but at last they remember the feathers. Standing on them, they are quickly lifted to safety just as the rock jaws slam shut.

We could identify with that story, having stood many times on slot rims with knees turning to rubber. Something about that bright edge dropping into deep blackness creates a dizzy insecurity, as if anything could happen.

Other stories tell of chindi — wandering ghosts, unfriendly spirits representing the bad, unbalanced parts of a person who has died. Caught between life and the afterlife, they haunt dark times and dark places. Slot canyons, naturally.

We found such stories only in books not written by Navajos. No one on the reservation warned us about spooky things. Their advice was more practical. That little van, it will get stuck in the sand. If you had a truck you wouldn't have to walk so far. What are you going to do if it rains? Flash floods are pretty dangerous. You know, rain wakes up the mud. Then the roads get slick and you can be stuck for days. Snakes fall in those slots, and can't get out. You might step on one in the dark. That would be too bad. It's a long way to the clinic.

Searching through a stack of aerial photos one year, we found the deepest slot we know of. It appeared as a ragged black line several miles long, running nearly straight through a sandy plain covered with desert scrub. It took us a full day following dirt tracks and an inadequate map to get within walking range, then several miles to the rim of the slot.

Working the angles amid frozen sandstone waves, Jeremy looks for a precarious perch for his camera and tripod.

It was a classic — hidden in the surrounding desert scrub, slightly flared in the upper 50 feet yet nearly invisible until we stood at the edge. I dropped my pack and, climbing gingerly across the sloping rock, scrambled to where one wall nearly touched the other. At that point, I could straddle the slot, one foot on each wall, and look straight down. A few dragon's teeth glowed dimly near the top, then all was black. Testing the depth, I dropped a stone into the maw. It hit early and shattered in a long echoing clatter. I tried other stones, searching for a place with an uninterrupted drop to the bottom. After six or eight tries, one fell true. It fell for eight seconds. The report, when it finally came, was not the sound of rock hitting rock but rather a splash, deep and resonant. A distant war drum. Code for Keep Out, but for Pat, who scrambled around slot canyons with a loose-jointed ease that I found hard to watch, it was an invitation. He strung a climbing rope from a juniper tree, tied a knot in the end to keep himself from slipping off into oblivion, stepped over the edge and disappeared. I could hear his boots and clothing scraping on the rock walls, but I couldn't see him. Soon the sound stopped.

"Holy shit," his voice echoed from the gloom.

"Does it reach?" I leaned over with one hand on the taut rope.

Silence. Minutes went by.

"Hey! Did you fall asleep?"

Distorted, demented sounds rose from the dark.

"Can you see the bottom?"

More scraping sounds. Heavy breathing.

At last he emerged from below the ledge. He had reached the end of the rope still far above the bottom. He had hung there for several long minutes, one foot against the rock to keep from spinning, peering into the dark but seeing only glimmers and shadows. It was still a long way to the bottom, he said, and as black as a bad dream.

We walked up-canyon along the rim for about a mile to a place we could enter by down-climbing. The canyon there was a mere 50 feet deep, the bottom so narrow we had to exhale to get through the constrictions. Yet the sculpting was gorgeous and the light was perfect. For several hours we moved along, slowly dragging cameras with us, entranced by what we had found. After three hours, we came to a stop at the edge of a big drop, water in a pool 30 feet below and no way of knowing how deep it was, but it looked like the kind of place we'd have to swim. Beyond it, only gloom, doom and wandering chindi. We stood silently at the drop for a long time, contemplating what might lie ahead, thinking about how to rig a rappel rope, knowing we couldn't take cameras into those deep shadows without waterproof cases, never mind what we would need for ourselves.

"Not me," said Pat, which meant there would be no volunteers. We turned and headed back.

In those several hours, we had hauled our gear perhaps 400 yards, a short distance for a lot of effort. Dragging it back to the surface, we talked about the chances of exploring the entire canyon to its mouth, a distance of several miles. You'd want dry suits for the cold, ropes to get over the drops, stone bolts to serve as rappel anchors in the smooth rock, headlamps, waterproof bags, food, a modest supply of insanity and maybe more than one day. That's a shivery thought. It might require a night out — or rather, a night in, in a slot where it is midnight at noon, where the bottom isn't dry, where a flat space to lie down might not exist and where there's no escape from a flash flood. We would have to think about that. The trip would be a hard one, we decided, but it could be done.

Not me.

Somewhere down in the cave-like cold, illuminated only by glimmers of ricocheting light, Pat dangled at rope's end, spinning slowly, still far above the bottom, suspended in the convoluted space between narrow rock walls, a spider dancing in the jaw of a dragon.

More than 40 years have passed since that winter in Yellowstone. Many things changed for the three of us: the women in our lives, our homes, our jobs. We didn't see each other as often as we once had. Wandering the world on a shoestring was easy, even on the incomes of freelance journalists, and we travelled farther afield than we would ever have thought possible.

A combination of climbing and caving gear, and some camera support devices of our own invention, helped us hang out in the upper reaches of what we called Raven's Roost, after the nest at the bottom of the picture.

None of us was home for more than about half of each year. Yet one thing remained a shared constant. Now and then, we convened in canyon country, joined by various friends and family. All of them helped shape our relation-

Pat and Baiba spontaneously chose to get married on the brink of a slot canyon with a small, intimate wedding entourage that included Janis Kraulis (with camera), Darragh and Dana Slaymaker and Paul Horn.

ships with the canyons, especially fellow photographers, including Tad Nichols, Dana Slaymaker, Janis Kraulis and Roger Vernon. Their visual approach to these places, and the excellent images they produced, enriched our own. Pat even got hitched to his sweetheart on the rim of one of his favourite canyons.

Although we learned the geography well, there was never an end to exploring, consulting maps and wondering where in God's great funhouse we had gotten to. The canyons lured us back year after year.

We continued to make pictures. Thousands of them. In four decades, individually or together, we published slot canyon photographs and articles in dozens of magazines worldwide. In all of them, we kept to Art's original policy.

We never revealed locations. We never gave real names. Other people did that, even going so far as to write guide-books to once secret and sacred places, some of which are now famously swamped with visitors.

Then, to our immeasurable regret, we lost Art. He was killed in a helicopter crash near his high mountain cabin, while teaching an avalanche safety course.

He left a big emptiness, the sort of emptiness that people with big hearts inevitably leave when they depart our lives. He also left a lot to remember him by, including his trove of photographs and films. They provide a visual chronicle covering decades of wandering, from Antarctica to the Andes, from British Columbia to the upper slopes of Mount Everest. Many are about mountains. Many others are about the southwestern desert and its subterranean wonders.

Looking at them now, along with our own collections — these accumulated images telling stories of so many miles and years wandering the canyons — we realize they are not only a document of the invasion of the pre-recreationist physical landscape; they also represent the chronology of a friendship — a friendship that found its focus and rejuve-nation in the shared pursuit of wild places.

More than 40 years further on, Art is gone. But the canyons remain. Sandstone and the deep blue desert sky. Rippling waters. The croaks of canyon tree frogs beneath delicate hanging gardens. The sweet cascading call of canyon wrens. Windstorms, rattlesnakes and cactus spines. At night, tiny streams flow in ribbons over smooth shelves. They pick up the moonlight and transform it to molten silver beneath impenetrably black slickrock walls. Stars wheel overhead. The canyons call gently to us as they always have done.

So you went to the Louvre: what did you see?
After the first artist, only the copyist.

— Terry and Renny Russell, *On the Loose*

The leaves of this well-known redbud tree have been photographed many times over the years, by acclaimed pros and amateurs alike, whereas the patch of desert varnish (opposite) has almost certainly been captured only one time.

These paired photos, taken at opposite ends of the day, help to illustrate how much the direction and quality of light can vary with weather and sun angle, and how careful attention to these subtle shifts permits the capture of strikingly different moods.

Beginning as a crack or groove in smooth sandstone, a slot grows, cut and polished by silt-laden water. The softest penetrates the hardest and leaves behind the mark of its passing – not the canyon walls, not the delicate carvings, not the sand collected in graceful rippled bars, not the fine clay drying and peeling like the bark of a sycamore. The mark of water's passing is less these things than it is the space between them; as the important part of a ceramic water jug is not the clay but the space it encloses; as a house may be defined by its walls of wood and glass, while the space inside is what makes it a home.

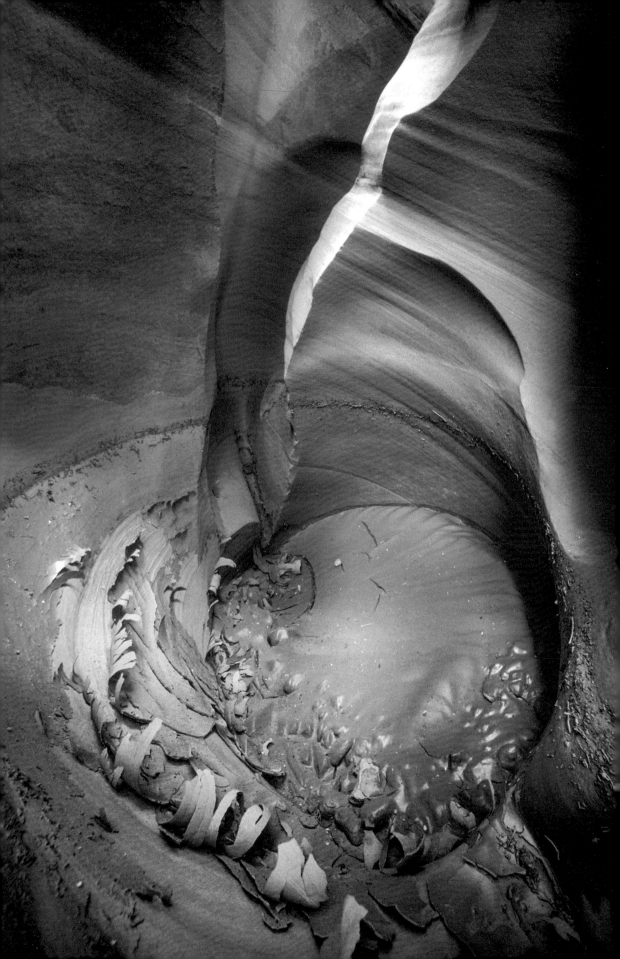

We live in a house that God built but that the former tenants re-modelled – blew up, it looks like – before we arrived. Poking through the rubble in our odd hours, we've found the corners that were spared and have hidden in them as much as we could. Not to escape from but to escape to: not to forget but to remember.

—Terry and Renny Russell, *On the Loose*

I don't think I could ever settle down. I have known too much of the depths of life already, and I would prefer anything to an anticlimax.

—Everett Ruess

Hollow reeds collect water from a tiny seep in the canyon wall.

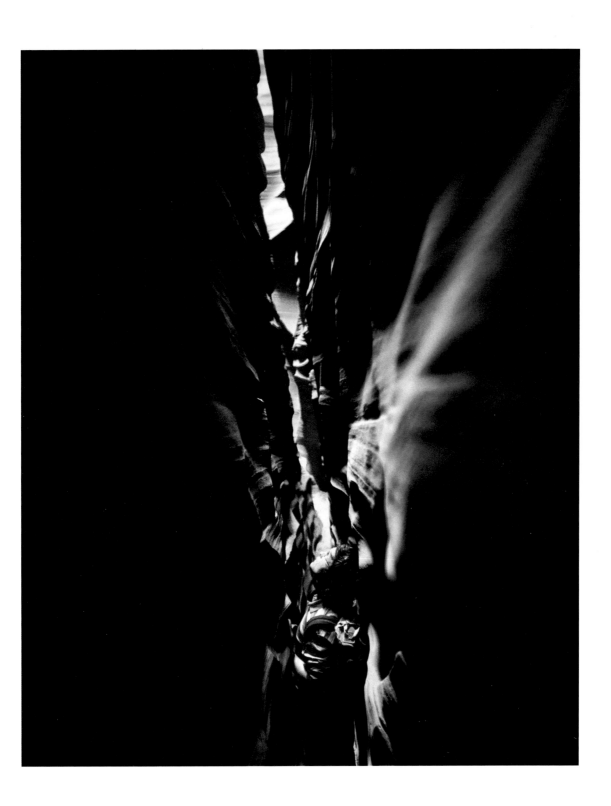

Not much wiggle
room in this slot.
Photo by Dana
Slaymaker.

Walk carefully with
open eyes. The
desert is a prickly
place whose exterior
belies a soft and
vivid heart.

Inspired by Paul Horn's music recorded in resonant spaces like the Taj Mahal, we invited him to explore the environment that provided the muse to Kokopelli (above), the wandering flute player, healer, symbol of fertility, spirit of music and common figure in petroglyphs throughout the southwest.

Canyons change and
remain the same. In the
1970s, water pouring
from a slot carved out
a perfect diving pool.
In recent years, flood-
carried sand and gravel
has made the pool too
shallow for diving – until
another flash flood brings
it back. Above, flood-
borne mud settles on
sand, then dries, cracks
and peels up in polygonal
plates. Footsteps destroy
them; floods renew them.

Testing the depth
with a hiking stick:
about five feet.

The most beautiful
fluted slots are also
the most fragile. To
avoid marking the
stone or damaging
delicate breakable
edges, we wore
white-crepe-soled
running shoes bought
at thrift stores.

Its substance [water] reaches everywhere; it touches the past and prepares the future; it moves under the poles and wanders thinly in the heights of air. It can assume forms of exquisite perfection in a snowflake, or strip the living to a single shining bone cast up by the sea.

—Loren Eiseley, *The Immense Journey*

Following pages: Art puts unwarranted faith in the friction of his cheap soles while Baiba trusts in the power of poetry.

Y ou have en-
tered a dream
world, an intricate
underground
fantasy where lines
bend, topsy meets
turvy, upside is
down, inside is out.
It makes as much
sense backward as
forward, which is
to say it makes no
sense at all.

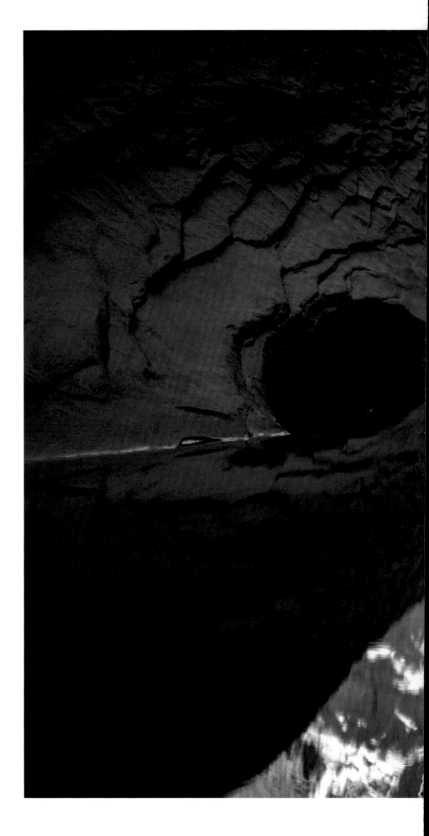

The next thing you'd see is this blue reflected from the sky, this beautiful, clear little pothole pool. Every little grotto was full of frogs and birds and wildflowers. Plus, the incredible light was what nearly drove us all crazy. There was no light in the world like that.

—Katie Lee

W ater moves fast through the canyons, soon gone. But where it lingers – in pools, springs and seeps – it seems abundant and generous. Canyon walls reflect the shapes of the water that carved them, and in their protective embrace the liturgy of water is celebrated with soft-spoken devotion.

Only sand
relentless dry earth
patient under flooding wash
The same sand
thirsty now,
the water's absence seems
incomprehensible.

A recent rainstorm
fills a creek with
fine mud, while clear
streams of water
from a "gusher"
seep pour through
a lush overhanging
garden of maidenhair
fern, columbine and
other moisture-loving
plants.

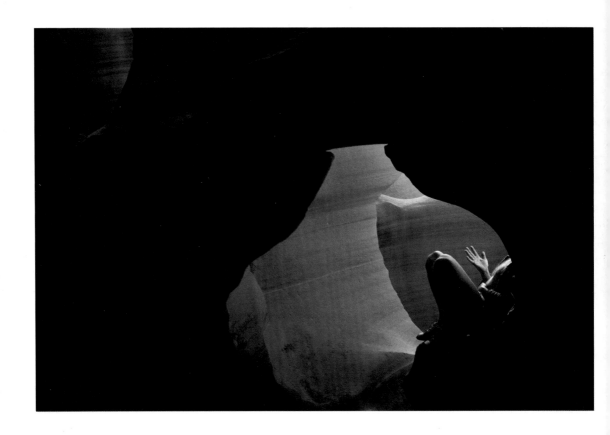

For in and out, above,
about, below,
'Tis nothing but a Magic
Shadow-show.

—Omar Khayyam
(trans. Edward FitzGerald)

He who fights with monsters should be careful lest he thereby become a monster. And if thou gaze long into an abyss, the abyss will also gaze into thee.

—Friedrich Nietzsche, *Beyond Good and Evil*

It is frightening,
a fearful place,
a place of death.

It is wide-mouthed.
It is narrow-mouthed.
It has mouths that pass through.

It is deep,
a difficult,
a dangerous place.
It is dark, it is light.

It is an abyss.

                                —Aztec definitions

After a hard day at work, Art emerges from an ornately carved slot, intent on a cold beer and yet another meal of tortillas and beans.

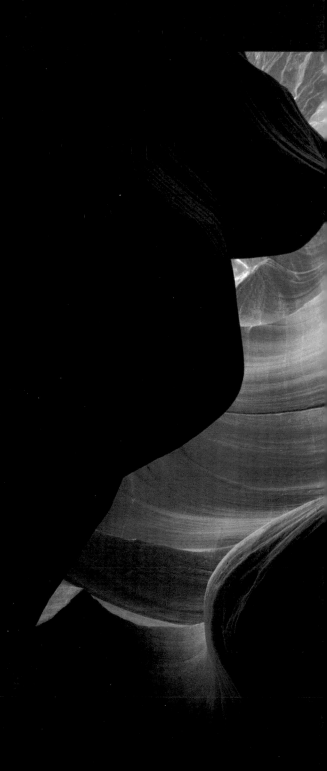

Its beauty stirs the imagination, and I wonder if the last refuge of all that is truly wild lies not on earth but in light.
—Ellen Meloy,
Eating Stone

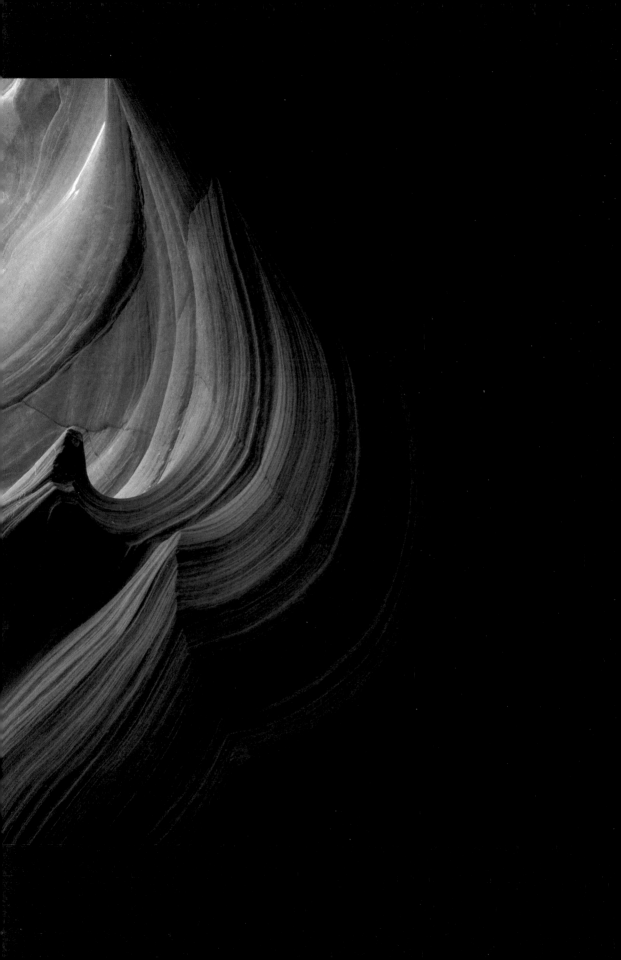

This is a place where things die. A gopher snake lay curled and cold in a pothole – fallen or washed in, doomed to slow starvation or violent death in a flash flood. So we moved it to a larger canyon with grass and trees and abundant packrats. We had done the snake a favour, we thought, and never mind how the packrats might take it. A week later we found it dead, a shrivelled corpse in the sand.

On his last foray into canyon country, Art's mentor,
photographer Tad Nichols,
peers into the magical world
to which he introduced Art.
Above, the sharp-edged
tools of the desert sculptor
include wind-driven sand,
here sifting down from the
rim like a dry waterfall.

Clear waters of a
permanent stream
slip gently through
one slot; in another,
mud curls tell of the
brief, violent ap-
pearance of a flash
flood where water
rarely flows.

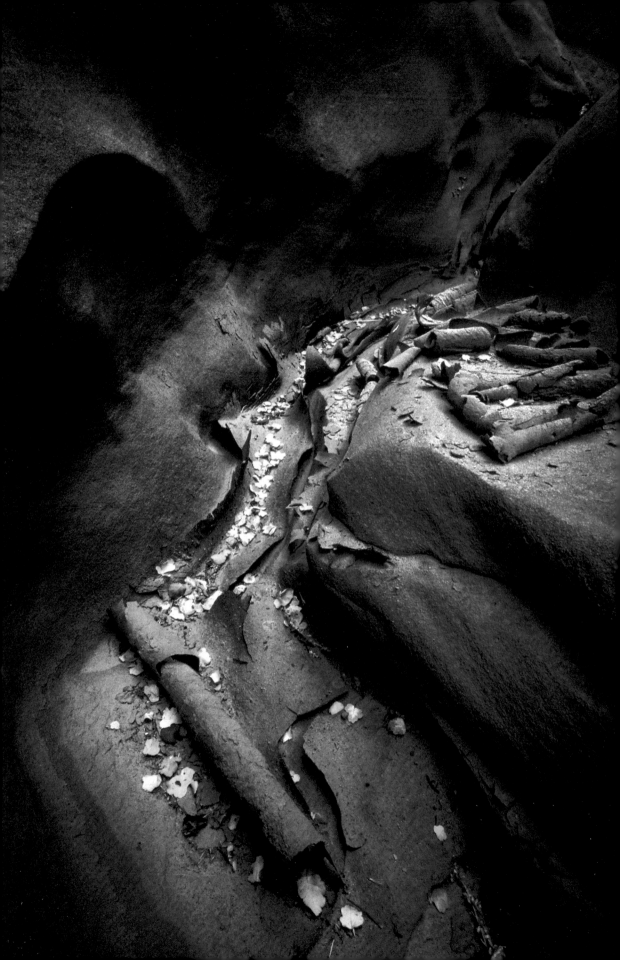

The marks of ancient people who lived and travelled here long before us are constant reminders that we are not the first to appreciate the cool shelter of the canyons. Following pages: Raven's Roost.

Aeolian sand
sifted
in layers
speaks of ancient winds
and how they blew.
Water,
cutting,
reveals in the rock
petrified wind.

Floors are never flat,
walls never straight.
Chambers large and
small, separated by
dry waterfalls, spiral-
ling chutes, arches
and tunnels, could be
rooms in the playhouse
of a child's fantasy.

Conservationist David Brower called Lake Powell "a huge reservoir, absolutely not needed in this century, almost certainly not needed in the next, and conceivably never to be needed at all." We occasionally, reluctantly, rented a motorboat to reach side-canyons we could then explore by kayak and on foot. Photo (right) by Dana Slaymaker.

Datura, or moonflower, blooming anew every night, nurtures a poisonous, hallucinogenic heart. The Navajo Generating Station, whose fumes colour the air throughout canyon country and penetrate the most remote crevices, purveys the products of a more deadly heart. Built in the 1970s, the coal-fired plant is slated to close in 2019.

An enterprising artifact salesman did not complete the act of removing a petroglyph from its native rock. Right: vandals had temporary success in an easily accessible canyon. Now a major tourist attraction and a Navajo Tribal Park, the canyon has been carefully restored to its natural state.

TAO
Canyon

Mid-afternoon. Sprawled in the warm shade of my van, I lean against my pack, dribbling sand between my fingers, watching toward the east. My friends are late. No matter. It's a fine day and a hot one, with nothing important to do except stay in the shade as it moves around the van. The desert is a liquid shimmer of heat waves. I have no reason to be out there in it.

I pull another can of beer from the cooler. Only two left, beside a forlorn sliver of ice. The beer foams up, runs over onto the sand, swallowed instantly. Cold beer in the summer desert? Drink it fast.

A puff of red dust appears in the distance, coming at me. Through binoculars I can see just ahead of the dust a white VW bus. The infamous White Whale, coming fast, risking its tired springs. Out here on the Navajo reservation I know it can't be anyone but Art blowing in from his home in British Columbia. All day I've seen nothing moving but Navajo pickups — some battered and worn, others with chrome stacks, whip antennas and jumbo tires — but every one a pickup. No Navajo would willingly drive that relic hippy-wagon the Whale.

The end of the road. From here it's a dense, intriguing, convoluted, ultimately satisfying slickrock puzzle, to be solved only by walking.

Art wanted to sell it before this trip. Sell it and buy a
Ford, an F-150 pickup, maybe a 250 — something that
wouldn't break down with such random frequency. Last
year just a few miles from here, the transaxle failed. We
spent three days camped on the roadside like a bunch of
Bedouin, rebuilding a shattered mess of gears. One day we
dismantled it. The next, someone hitched a ride to Flagstaff
and back for parts. The third day it rained while we put it
all back together. During that time, a few Navajos drove
by. Most waved in a friendly we-know-what-that's-about
manner. Some would stop to check out the work and make

VW maintenance, desert dirtbag style, with help from that essential book, *How to Keep Your Volkswagen Alive: A Manual of Step by Step Procedures for the Compleat Idiot.* The White Whale needed a new transaxle.

knowing comments about old cars, rough roads and back-country mechanics before climbing back into their pickups. They did it kindly, without snarky chortles, but you could see it in their eyes, and Art got the message. "I've had it. I'm finished," he said. "I want a truck."

Yet here it comes again, the old white van, and the sight gives me pleasure. Last winter I found one for myself, slightly newer than his, also white and no less cranky. We cursed the sand and the rain and the heat and the stubborn greasy gears last year, but down deep we must have liked knowing we could take care of ourselves and our battered machines.

The Whale skids to a halt. Art climbs out, toothy grin showing through a huge black beard tinged red by a coating of dust. With him are two other Canadians down to soak up some desert heat: Pat is with him, and also Bernhard Ehmann, a swarthy rock climber who greets me with a German accent and the sort of handshake that could come in handy if you wanted to remove lug nuts without a wrench. Art knew what he was doing when he invited Bernhard.

There will be yet another white vehicle along before the day is over — Kay and Tuck Forsythe, from Moab, Utah, in their antique Chevy Carryall, the one that blew out its wiring last winter in a fit of nervous circuitry disorder. That happened in a place where Tuck didn't mind staying a week, which was good because he spent day after day running little wires through little holes to get the old beast running again. Like the rest of us, he and Kay can live on almost nothing if they do most things for themselves — our sort of freedom. Freedom costs either time or money, and for the young, time is the easier to come by.

We expect them sometime over the next few hours, give or take half a day. Anything might slow them down. An unusual petroglyph panel could take hours; they like trying to decipher the meanings behind ancient rock art. Or they might spend time slowly chasing a lizard they can't identify. Maybe they just pull over for a nap under a shady rock ledge. Punctuality, for all of us, is overrated.

And nothing to worry about. Near dark, they roll in, trailing a cloud of their own. Kay, the all-around naturalist, her pockets stuffed with plant bits, her brain full of species names and the private ways of desert creatures, carries a notebook bulging with pressed blossoms she picked along the way. She is effervescent in her greetings. Tuck, the ever-thoughtful math-brain, is correspondingly quiet. Words come slowly to Tuck because he never wants to say anything imprecisely. Ask him a question and you might wait long seconds for an answer. As he forms a response you might think he is ignoring you, but as far as I can tell, Tuck has never ignored anything. If you want to know what he thinks, patience is a requirement, and it's usually worth the wait.

There's no waiting the next morning. We set off early, in the first glimmer of light. Our way leads across open desert, weaves through scratchy blackbrush shrubs, drops down a ravine into a broad valley and then up a seemingly endless miles-long dry wash. We start before dawn to avoid the heat, while knowing it really can't be avoided. Sure enough, by mid-morning it is fully upon us. April can be pleasant on the Colorado Plateau, filled with the freshness of spring. Or it can bring the oven blasts of midsummer. This could be July. Air, 95 Fahrenheit. Sand, 120 and getting hotter. The cheerful banter of early morning disappears in weary silence.

The wash heats up like an oven, but climbing up out of it gains us nothing. The terrain on either side is worse — a junkyard of hills and gullies, sharp ledges, loose gravel, prickly-pear cactus and blackbrush, thick and sharp-branched so you can't walk through it without tearing your legs. The wash might be blazing hot, but at least it's a smooth path.

If only it weren't a path of soft sand. The sand rolls underfoot. There's no traction, nothing to push against. If you try to walk normally, your foot just slips backward. So you walk flat-footed, short-stepping with an odd vertical movement. Heat or no heat, it's awfully tiring to walk in soft sand.

But we have a goal. It is a good goal, we are pretty sure of that, and we have a rough idea how to get there. Our goal is a big canyon with a clear stream and old cottonwood trees in shady alcoves. A few years ago, one of our desert rat friends tried to get into it from the opposite direction, entering near the canyon's mouth. She found the way blocked by pools and waterfalls and quicksand. Impassible, she said, alluring but impassible — and she was not a person to be turned back by small obstacles.

We've already seen it from above, on aerial survey photos — black-and-white stereo pictures that showed the relative depths and steepness of canyon walls. Topographic maps can't do that. In slot country, contour lines skip across narrow chasms with hardly a jitter, and where walls hundreds of feet high overhang the canyon bottom, contour lines simply disappear. They have nothing to report because the map maker can't see below the overhang.

Photos are better, and rangers at the local Park Service office were eager to help when we told them what we were after. They brought out thick files of black-and-white prints that we spread across the floor of the map library and assembled into a mosaic. We went after our canyon with magnifying glasses, carefully keying features in the photos with those on our topographic maps. There it was — a meandering black slit surrounded by barren rock. Other slits fed into it, forming a huge branched pattern of enigmatic shadowed lines, too dark for us to see any details within them. Yet here and there, a slit widened ever so slightly, giving us a glimpse of a stream flowing on a sandy bottom. And then, the best: the tops of cottonwood trees, just the upper branches of leafy trees, appeared hundreds of feet below the rim.

Scientists poring over Mars photos and finding furry little tails sticking out from under rocks wouldn't be more excited than we were. There it was, proof of hidden life and light and space. The canyon was big, with generous carved-out hollows where things could grow. Things as big as trees. That meant birdsong. Wildflowers. Lizards and frogs and praying mantises and who knew what else.

We decided to call it Tao Canyon for a couple of reasons. Tao was a good-sounding word, and it called to mind the poem by Laozi, in the *Tao Te Ching*:

> Thirty spokes share the wheel's hub;
> It is the center hole that makes it useful.
> Shape clay into a vessel;
> It is the space within that makes it useful.
> Cut doors and windows for a room;
> It is the holes that make it useful.
> Therefore profit comes from what is there;
> Usefulness from what is not there.
>   (trans. Gia-Fu Feng and Jane English)

Rock without space within it is just rock. Space without rock to give it shape is just space. To be meaningful, each needs the other. Laozi could have been writing about slot canyons.

Especially the one that "is not there." Beyond the ones we

A slot seen from above is the calligraphy of water written in stone. Before the days of online satellite imagery, we could scout from the air with the help of a local pilot and his Cessna. A view like this showed a potentially good slot and gave us a reference point for finding it on foot.

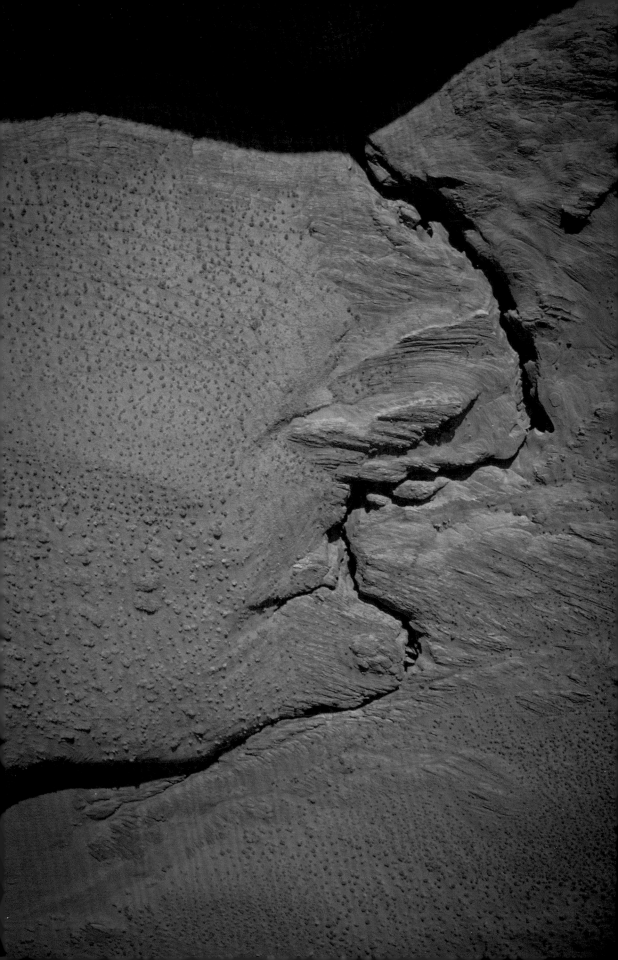

Out of reach in plain sight, a huge slot canyon seems as impenetrable as a dream. Getting there is an act of faith. Or of seduction, the direct approach being a sure path to failure.

could find, we thought of Tao Canyon more as an archetype than an actual place — a sort of slickrock Xanadu, a Platonic ideal. Search forever but you will never find it, and in any case, finding it would be a kind of defeat, proof of the ideal's non-existence. Then the search would be over, done in by anticlimax. Although we called it Tao, and hoped for great things, we knew this one, like every other one, could never be the Tao of our minds.

By two in the afternoon we cross a low ridge and find ourselves on the edge of it. The canyon — or rather, what we know to be the canyon's drainage, a very large area — lies ahead. Every ravine, every crack in the rock, every incipient slot, leads into it, downhill from here, and that feels good. We're almost there.

Too bad we're not.

We can't find it. Not the actual canyon. We can't mistake the canyon. Together with its tributaries, it covers a hundred square miles of domes, pinnacles, overhanging cliffs, perched ledges and dead ends. Once we cross into Tao's drainage, it's everywhere around us, unavoidable. But also impenetrable. We have entered a kind of reverse maze where instead of walls, hundreds of slots lie in our path. Walking along the rim of one leads only to the rim of another, each one sloping into a dark unseen bottom. A couple of hours of trying to move in a downstream direction, and we have to admit it. We are stuck.

To understand, picture the veins of a maple leaf, an enormous leaf miles across. Imagine the veins sunken into the rock as if, heated to incandescence, they had melted into it to form an intricate system of barriers. You can't step across any but the smallest ones far out on the perimeter. Now try to find a walking path from the tip of the leaf to the main stem. It's almost impossible.

Sussing out the photo potential around the next bend requires either swimming or some delicate rock climbing moves – or both, if you happen to slip.

Entry-level
canyoneering:
start at the
top.

These little, little slits aren't what we came for. They aren't beautifully fluted and shaped. Instead, they're dark and uninviting. For a while we try to get around them on the surface, but in the end there's only one obvious choice: follow the water. Water built this strange place. Follow it. Go where the water goes, down off the slickrock into the slots.

It should be simple. Pick a slot — any one, they all lead to the same place. Follow the cool semi-caverns to the great canyon beyond. We have ropes and climbing gear for the inevitable drop-offs. We don't mind swimming across the pools we know are down there, and we might even like swimming. We're hot, getting grumpy, ready for some shade. So without much argument, we scramble into the nearest body-width crack to see where it leads.

Slots are carved mostly by the violence of flash floods, not the gentle action of smoothly flowing streams. Their floors are almost never flat, nor smooth. They can be too narrow for a single foot, so your shoes don't have anything solid to stand on. You have to avoid cramming them into a V-shaped, ankle-busting crack, but then a few yards farther the floor drops away entirely, down to murky darkness. If the walls stay close enough at this point, and they are not too slippery with mud, you might be able to chimney your way downward, bridging the walls with legs spread as wide as needed, or with hands against one wall and feet against the other. That works until the space gets too wide. Now you need a rope, and what do you anchor that to?

To boulders, sometimes. Boulders huge and small roll down from above, jam themselves into the narrows and make pretty good anchors. Others are a mess. Debris of all kinds — sticks, logs, smaller stones, sand, dead animals — falls into canyons, or is carried by floods, and piles up against the boulders. Climbing over the piles, you face undercut drop-offs, and again, out come the ropes. As you make your way down the ropes tied to log jams, the disturbed sand and other shit (literally) rains down out of the debris, covering you with god-knows-what. Then, as if to make up for the discomfort, the bottom widens out with false promise, wide enough to have a walkable floor. Your spirits lift. You think the canyon is opening, that you'll come around a bend to an ever-enlarging space where instead of collecting in these filthy pools the water will flow, and the

Following pages: Trying to find a way into a deep slot that doesn't require a rope, Pat tests the limits of friction.

In soft mud and cold water the imperative is to keep gear dry, while bracing oneself for a submerged, invisible drop-off.

The earth opens
its jaws just
enough
        to admit
the width of
shoulders
Squeeze between
sharp
interlocking
        teeth.
They block the view
ahead
A crooked line
Deeper
        deeper
into coolness
smoothness
coldness
rockness.

water will be clear and sun-warmed from passing through bright alcoves. So on you go to the next disappointment: the lip of a new pit. This lip is slick with mud and the pit holds a cold, darkly glimmering pool. Beyond the pool, apparently, there's only more of the same.

We know it can be like that, but we try anyway. At first the slot is dry. Soon we come to standing water, so we take our boots off and put on sneakers. Next we slide into deeper water, and off come pants, then packs, to be carried above our heads. There are drop-offs. The first ones we scramble down; others require a rope for assistance, but they aren't big drops, not yet. Where the walls pinch together too tight even for our shoulders, we turn sideways, hauling packs behind us. Gradually, the deeper we go, the less we see of the sky, until it's only a thin ribbon glimpsed occasionally.

Two hours of this and we've made perhaps half a mile. We're beginning to think we picked the wrong slot. This one is staying awfully narrow, and it's just getting darker. Enthusiasm withers. So, shivering from cold, we grunt our way back to the surface via a smaller side-slot that joins the one we've been struggling through. The heat feels good now and we soak it up like chilled lizards.

Onward across the warped pavement of sandstone: a rock wilderness of domes and spires.

No trees, no shade, but there is water, a little bit of it, caught in pools from the last rain, days ago, lingering now but evaporating, and only a few inches deep. The water is warm, a little greasy to the touch, getting green with algae, filled with life. Horsehair worms, eight inches long and thick as a bowstring, wriggle horribly, but they are harmless to humans. Water striders jet across the surface as we approach, alarmed but with nowhere to go. In some pools, tree frogs sing loudly while clutching each other

It was the sweetest, most mysterious-looking place any one could imagine.... It seemed almost like being shut out of the world in some fairy place.

—Frances Hodgson Burnett, *The Secret Garden*

In low light levels our time exposures ranged from seconds to minutes long, giving us opportunities to play with figures that dropped out of frame part way through the exposure, creating ghost images.

Barefoot cookery at
the mouth of a slot.

in a mating frenzy. Their eggs, in gelatinous strings, slip
from our fingers as we try to pick them up. Tadpoles are
already hatched, but what chance do they have, coming
from parents who laid eggs in the face of such uncertainty?
The pools are ephemeral. Without rain, they will be gone
like footprints in the sand, dried up and all frog song blown
away on hot wind.

Evening finds us still wandering on the dizzy sandstone,
poking into every crack that looks like it might go somewhere, but none is promising enough to explore. Everyone
is disoriented despite frequent arguments over the useless
map. Tempers rise with the heat. Six different opinions and
each one right.

Bloody hell, how do we get there?

Look, way down below the big dome, is that a
cottonwood?

Where?

Maybe.

How far is it, do you think?

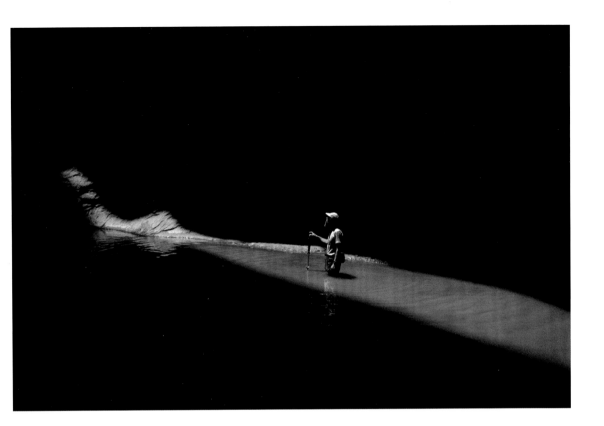

We won't get there today.

What if we went up on the bench, up there in the black-brush? Wouldn't it be easier going?

Sure, but it wouldn't get you near the canyon.

I'm going back the other way.

But we're so close. There has to be a way in.

We find a place to camp, a smooth stone shelf perched on the edge of a slot — not very deep, and well supplied with the best water we can find, meaning another algae-slicked pool, the ugly but drinkable home to swarms of minute creatures. Water with a protein content. Canyon soup: just boil and serve.

"You know," says Art, "pothole water makes a pretty fair drink if you dump it out and fill your cup with whisky." It's an old joke, but as true as a sunrise.

Morning brings renewed energy and a new plan: go light, go fast. Stripping to shorts and T-shirts, carrying ropes and not much else, we plunge into a new slot, determined

Art warms himself in a narrow shaft of light beaming down from the noon-scorched rim a hundred feet above the cold, shadowed pool in which he stands.

to stop for nothing. After all, we have come to see what's here. We feel a strong curiosity about what is certainly one of the strangest places on Earth. Might as well take it whole hog.

Bernhard, the independent Teuton, wants nothing of that, and charges off on his own. His plan is to circle around the edge of the maze, hoping to find the lower canyon.

"You might find it," someone says, "but you won't be able to get into it. The walls are too high down there."

Heated argument. Off he goes, alone.

The rest of us descend into the gloomiest dungeon yet. Without water it would be merely unattractive, but this is springtime, meaning the pools are full. We sink to our chests. Twice we swim. The water is icy, our feet numb. Shattered trunks of juniper trees, draped with mucky debris, hang above us, jammed in by floods. We pass a black widow spider, mired in the mud, upside down, legs moving feebly, red spot up, warning.

There are no serious obstacles until, thinking we're making progress, we edge around a sharp bend into a jug-shaped chamber with a muddy chute in its floor, a dark hole that goes down like a water slide, descending to near blackness. We hesitate, shivering with cold, peering into it, seeing a glimmer of water 15, maybe 20 feet below — a long way to uncertainty. No one seems willing to move until Tuck, typically quiet with thoughts of his own, sits on the stone chute and, without a word, lets himself go. Gone from sight. Big cannonball splash. Swimming sounds. Then his weirdly echoing voice telling us to come on as he climbs out on the far side of the pool.

"What's down there?"

"Water."

Are you swimming?

"Standing in mud."

"Can we make it back up?"

"Why not?" Hypothermic reasoning. To make sure, we string a rope from a jammed boulder and follow him down.

After that comes a long stretch of muddy pools and vaulted chambers so dim we should have brought flashlights. It's hard to stand upright, struggling for footing in the ooze. The water is knee-deep, waist-deep, sometimes deeper. There is no dry ground, almost no ground, muddy or not, to climb out onto.

The canyon deepens, the sky only occasionally visible, the walls wildly convoluted. Beautiful? Interesting to photograph? None of us think of it. Gusts of wind at the desert surface sound a roar suggestive of flash floods. This isn't thunderstorm season, but that becomes a thought of diminishing reassurance. We can't see the sky. How would we know?

In the yin and yang of a difficult canyon, Paddy O'Reilly ponders the wholeness of opposites (that shadow cannot exist without light). Or maybe he's just trying to find a way out.

Then comes the worst: the walls, instead of rising vertically, slant at a steep angle, one side like a sloping roof, the other a sloping floor. We cannot walk upright. We have to bump along on our shoulders and hips, leaning steeply to the left, the right wall close above us. The water deepens with the darkness, and soon we find ourselves trying to swim in that position, stretching our toes for any purchase that might exist, pushing with our arms. Then there is something clutching at our feet, something sharp, entangling and thought provoking. And beyond it, another chute, bigger than the one Tuck threw himself down. That's the end. Determination flickers and goes out. Once again, back the way we came.

Late in the afternoon, Bernard returns discouraged. He has been to a point where he could look down into a wide spot in the canyon, water flowing, trees growing — the nirvana we know is there. It's there, but he could find no way in.

"We could rappel into it, maybe."

Bad idea. Art climbed out of a canyon one time, ascending a rope he had rappelled down several hours earlier. He came over the rim to see a packrat in the act of chewing his rope; already it had severed the sheath and was working on the inner fibres — and thus his life — as he came into view.

Where is Tao Canyon? Again the maps come out. An argument develops — a sluggish one, delivered from prone positions with no great emotion. Some want to spend the rest of the day here; others want to get on, to hell with the heat. Art finally gets up and starts toward higher slickrock. We all follow.

We travel until dusk, all the while probing, retracing our steps, trying new directions, moving on, ever down-canyon, until we encounter a huge and complex side-canyon that blocks our way and forces a decision — and another disagreement. Pat and Bernhard have had enough of the sewers. They decide to strike off at dawn for the lower reaches of the canyon, going up and around, hoping that by a long desert hike they will find a way into the broader stretches below. The rest of us think it's better to look this place over and perhaps launch another attempt into the disreputable deeps. On one thing we agree. It's time for another camp on bare rock. We find a patch of soft sand for sleeping, and wood for boiling slot water. It's an improvement, and a sort of omen.

There is a truth known to every serious bird watcher and Zen student that applies to any fervent search for things rare and elusive. Pursuit is self-defeating. When you stop looking — that is, when you are no longer aggressively stalking — you have a better chance of finding. Only then does the object of desire allow itself to be found, if it is to be found at all.

So it happens with Tao Canyon. After another morning of fruitless probing, the consensus shifts. We should have followed Pat and Bernhard when they left at dawn. They had the right idea after all. We could start now. If we do, we can make a few miles before dark. No one disagrees, and so, resigned to it, we begin, heading out and up away from the canyon. And then, there it is, suddenly in sight below us. A weakness, a ramp of broken rock, leads to the canyon bottom down a fracture in the wall, a rubbly ladder all the way down.

Meanwhile, Pat and Bernhard were also right. After a two-hour hike through the open desert, they find a similar break in the rim at the canyon's lower end. Two days later, somewhere between those two ramps, we meet them in the canyon bottom, big-eyed and grinning.

Tao proves to be the hidden treasure we'd hoped for.
Surrounded by desert, protected by the baffling maze of
its own making, it could be its own world, a sort of alien
implant set into the floor of a completely opposite landscape. Other canyons like it do exist, a handful at least,
some well known, some more accessible, perhaps more
spectacular. But to us, resting on its sandy bottom, having
seen no footprints but our own, it becomes our personal
Eden, a secret garden behind a hidden gate.

We walk in a clear stream flowing shallow over red
sand beneath giant walls. There is just the right amount of
vegetation, planted as if by design in a series of enormous multicoloured arcing-overhead conch shells, their
upper edges set apart just far enough to let in shafts of
theatrical light.

It's springtime. Cottonwoods produce gentle seed-
bearing snow. Long gelatinous strands of amphibian eggs
undulate in every quiet pool. Tiny willow sprouts cover
the sandbars. Every leaf of every plant is new green, the

Water decorates
the canyon. A maple
tree finds just enough
moisture to thrive
against a blue-
varnished wall that
was once a wind-
blown dune. Right: a
slow seep paints a
natural tapestry with
leached minerals.

special brilliant green made even brighter by red-hued light reflected off the sandstone walls. Frogs are mating. So are the water striders and dragonflies and hornets. Lizards are too, judging from the way they play reptile grab-ass, chasing each other wildly across the rocks.

The creek is small with a slow, clear current that lingers in pools deep enough to soak in but not for swimming, and the perfect temperature for a hot afternoon. We slip into the pools and sit neck-deep among the tree frogs. We call them canyon peepers. They were singing here, before we came along and shut them up. Soft-bodied little things with round pads on their toes and yellow stripes on the insides of their thighs, they start up the chorus again if we stay quiet. Some sound like sheep, others like wheels needing oil, or frogs tormented, squeezed through places too tight even for frogs. Mating madness in the frog world is the sound of mingled bliss and anguish.

We spend a night in a place where old cottonwood trees crowd thickly into a section of canyon wide enough that floods, when they come, spread out and lack the force to uproot the trees. It is a jungle of vegetation, hard to move through, tall grasses over our heads, dense shrubs and tangled branches. The humidity is palpable, packing in thick and heavy like the insects here, like the trees and cattails and birds. I stay awake long into the night, watching the moonlight filter through leaves overhead and listening to frogs shrieking from their little pools. There are reptiles, too — we've seen leopard lizards, fence lizards, collared lizards, side-blotched lizards, striped whiptails, gopher snakes, rattlesnakes, racers, horned toads and others — seemingly hundreds of them, judging by the noise they make racing through the dried leaves that cover the ground; and never mind the packrats, mice, scorpions, centipedes and other things that emerge in the night. Running and

Previous pages: Tao Canyon was the perfect hidden garden tended only by the natural cycle of the seasons.

Right: Years after this picture was made, Art returned and witnessed a flash flood in these narrows. In two minutes, he reported, the stream grew from two inches deep and five feet across to five feet deep and 30 feet wide. The water was icy cold, opaque with sediment and heavily laden with floating debris.

sliding through the clattering leaves, they sound for all the world like things much bigger: bears, moose, crazed coyotes, chindi. In the moonlight, you can imagine anything. I sleep poorly, but it is not unpleasant. There is too much going on around me to wish I were asleep.

Another night we are far down-canyon, where the walls rise much higher — higher and grander than any of us have seen before. There are no trees here; in fact hardly anything at all grows here. The canyon bottom is flat, bare sand between immense rock walls. It's nothing more than an aisle, a water passage nearly dry now, but a violent river during floods. In the narrows below it we find the only tree, a battered trunk 50, maybe 100 feet above the stream, wedged across the canyon, its limbs torn away. The cottonwood carcass speaks to us of savage waters, and we can't help but feel some fear.

On a third night the wind rises and prowls the desert above. At first we hear a heavy organ-like moaning as it leaps the gap of the canyon and tears itself apart on sharp pinnacles. Small stones, dislodged 400 feet above, rocket into the sand around us. Later, wind gusts find their way to the canyon floor, screaming first one way and then the other like trapped spirits seeking a way out. They carry clouds of sand, blasting us head and foot, filling our sleeping bags and hair and ears with grainy grit. Sweltering in the bags, hoods pulled over our heads and drawstrings tight, it starts to feel personal, as if something is trying to drive us mad. We scramble for a rock ledge above the sand blizzard and find only partial respite.

In the morning we are weary and buffeted, but it doesn't matter. There is no need to go anywhere. We can sleep anytime, and some of us do.

Later in the day, we encounter a small and perfect waterfall with an equally perfect pool below it. I spend hours

Water in free fall sluices away the sand embedded in Art's hair and beard.

there, sitting first on its lip, letting the cold water play through my fingers, wondering at such a tiny stream in so large a canyon. Then I move below the falling ribbon, kneel on the rock rim and wash the windstorm sand out of my eyes. In this green and gently streaming grotto one expects to find an elf. Better, I find tiny lizards among the maiden-hair ferns. Sitting with my back against the curving rock, I watch the sky far above and the lengthening patch of sun sliding down the wall as the afternoon wears on. Soon the falls are brilliantly lit and the water warmed to bath temperature. I wade in, floating on my back with the spray spattering across my face.

One evening, Art and I crouch in the rubble below an enormous overhang, watching a tiny lizard hunt for flies and gnats. The lizard fails time after time. It's not the most genetically gifted of its species, we decide, and in a natural selection sort of way we should allow its sorry situation to play out. But we have sympathy for its hard work, and eventually we intervene, stunning flies with our hats and

The slots provide sanctuary for prickly-pear cactus, mariposa lilies and great horned owls alike.

tossing them toward the clumsy creature, which leaps and scrambles and pounces until bloated, and still it tries to cram flies back into its mouth as they crawl out.

Art asks me, "Are you getting hungry?"

"Nope."

Back at camp, Kay has brewed tea of rosemary mint, the purple sage of Zane Grey riders fame. It turns out to be a sedative. We barely make it to our sleeping bags.

The canyon stretches for miles, through wide places and narrow ones, some of the narrows as forbidding as those we saw on the first day, but always passable. In places, Tao is a yard wide at the bottom and over 100 yards deep, the sky not visible from the floor; but it always opens out again. Quicksand is common in the narrows, which makes only for some fast stepping, quicksand being one of the world's most overrated natural horrors.

No one wants to leave. Stretching our food, we turn five days into seven, taking psychic nourishment from the sight of cathedral-high tapestried walls, the brilliance of cottonwood leaves in the sun, the water of the stream warm on our bare feet, the sand clean and hot and dry on the floor of the alcoves. Breakfast might not happen until noon. Lunch substitutes for dinner. Hours pass as though they had never existed, and so do the days.

When we finally climb back to the rim country, it seems that we have been in the canyon for a long time. The return trip is shorter because we know the route. We have walked it, measured it with our feet, and now we understand a small part of that big landscape.

All afternoon clouds build over the mesa on the far side of Tao. They aren't enough to give us shade on the way out, but late in the day, as we climb the last long slope to where we left our cars, the clouds coalesce into a dark-bellied thunderhead, with lightning flickering and gouts of dust

A collared lizard perches atop a shard of burnt juniper trunk.

telling us of a turbulence we can't feel from so far away. Then it opens. Ragged curtains of rain fall at an angle to the ground, becoming a solid grey mass, obliterating our view of the mesa.

I know that in Tao, water is running down the slickrock walls, collecting in pools, overflowing and churning through the narrow caverns, over the hidden waterfalls, carving and smoothing and deepening. Earlier in the day, we passed isolated potholes filled with frogs' eggs but nearly dry. They will be overflowing now. Looks like a good year for the canyon peepers.

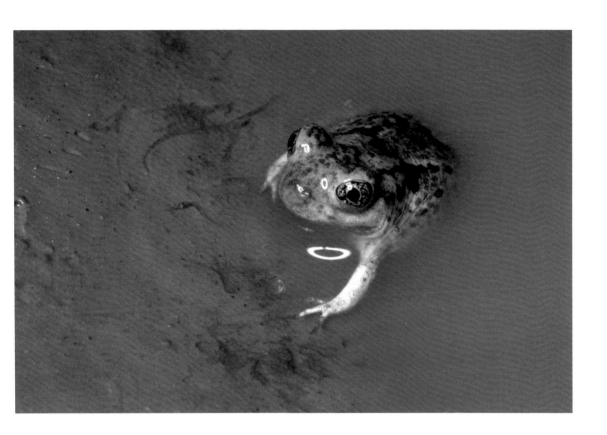

A spadefoot toad, actually a frog that looks like a toad, depends on intermittent floods for breeding. The sound of thunder brings spadefoots out from their underground shelters for a binge of puddle-stoked reproduction.

EPILOGUE

The world represented by this book — that glorious expanse of canyon-slashed red rock called the Colorado Plateau — has changed since we began our wandering partnership more than 40 years ago. It has become popular among people seeking recreation, well-travelled beyond anything we could have imagined, and therefore crowded. More regulated. Noisier. You need to join a lottery for permission to visit places that were once obscure and empty.

And it has not changed. Much of it remains as beautiful and filled with spirit as it ever has been, thanks to protection, management and regulation by various agencies charged with preventing us, collectively, from trampling the

Jeremy organizes his notebooks while Art blows sand out of his 4x5 camera, a crevice-filled device he came to call his sandbox.

place to dust. We might chafe — we do chafe — under the inconvenience of having to wait in line, yet the last thing we want is for these places to be unloved. It's an old argument that wild nature needs advocates, and a true one. Abbey said it well, in an essay published in the same 1974 calendar that carried the photograph by Art Twomey that opens this book: "The idea of wilderness needs no defense, it only needs defenders."

While recreational use has exploded, so have activities that have nothing to do with loving canyon country — or with not loving it for that matter, although these activities destroy it down to its heart. The landscape is incidental, a thing of no meaning, when it comes to exploitations like fracking, mining, over-pumping of ancient aquifers, abolishing protected areas (read, Bears Ears), trampling Native rights (read, the same) and so much more — the familiar litany of arrogance and loss.

We are mindful of our early mentors, the likes of Tad Nichols, Katie Lee, Frank Wright and David Brower who, a generation before us, loved a place — Glen Canyon — that was gone by the time we came on the scene. We knew how they felt about the drowning of a natural treasure that few people ever had a chance to appreciate, and yet we found other places, and everything we found was fresh and new to us. In all justice for all those searching for Tao Canyons of their own, that opportunity should never change.

But it can. Threats have only increased with the years. There's nothing new in saying we need to take a stand, resist short-sighted avaricious policy, reinforce existing protections and fight like rattlesnakes against the constant pressure to degrade what people before us have managed to protect. Those are old imperatives often repeated — repeated now more urgently than ever.

We could lose these places, even ones like national parks, whose protection seems assured through the weight of tradition and history. For even the parks survive at the whim of Congress, and that should make us all feel nervous. We certainly could lose these places, and we surely will, if we don't continue to fight for them.

ACKNOWLEDGEMENTS

We wish to thank all who patiently froze in their tracks while we recorded sometimes minutes-long exposures on low-sensitivity film in our tripod-mounted cameras, as well as those who provided inspiration and shared the thrill of discovery with us during more than ten years of canyon exploring. Among the most important of them is Margie Jamieson, Art's partner in life, who provided Art's original chromes and encouragement to finish what Art inspired so long ago.

Thanks also to Rocky Mountain Books: publisher Don Gorman for bringing this long-delayed project to fruition; and graphic artist Chyla Cardinal for giving our draft design a professional touch. We're grateful to Dana Slaymaker, companion on numerous trips into the slots, for his included images. Toronto Image Works provided tack-sharp scans of our 40-year-old Kodachromes.

Our apologies to a couple of people who appear in photos taken by Art who are unidentified — if you recognize yourselves we'd sure like to hear from you. The folks we know are listed here, unless already mentioned in a caption:

On the Cover: Baiba Morrow in the heart of it. Page 2 Pat rappels, Bernhard Ehmann belays; 24 Art; 38 Jeremy; 44 Margie, Art; 45 Art; 54 Pat; 70 Art; 72 Baiba; 73 Shirley Zaleschuk, Art, Phil Weatherspoon; 75 Jeremy; 77 Linda Kuttis, Janis Kraulis; 82 Liam O'Reilly?; 83 Pat; 84 Karen Paynter; 85 Linda, Janis; 95 Baiba; 96, 97 Art; 98 Bernhard; 101 Jean Dunwiddie; 102 Pat; 104 Margie, Marita Askey; 106, 107 Jeremy; 114 Jeremy; 122 Jeremy; 124 Jeremy, Dana Slaymaker; 125 Pat, Jeremy; 130/31 Pat; 134 Art; 140/41 Jean, Art; 143 Pat; 148/49 Bernhard; 153 Baiba; 154 Margie, Art; 162/63 Jean; 165 Jean, Jeremy; 179 Baiba; 182 Pat; 184 Wendy Baylor, Christy Bertani.

BOOKS WE LIKE

Glen Canyon: Images of a Lost World. Tad Nichols and Gary Ladd. Santa Fe: Museum of New Mexico Press, 1999.

All My Rivers Are Gone: A Journey of Discovery Through Glen Canyon. Katie Lee. Boulder, Colo.: Johnson Books, 1998.

On the Loose. Renny and Terry Russell. Salt Lake City, Utah: Gibbs-Smith, 2001.

The Anthropology of Turquoise: Meditations on Landscape, Art, and Spirit. Ellen Meloy. New York: Pantheon (hardcover), 2002.

Finding Everett Ruess. David Roberts. New York: Broadway Books, 2011.

Desert Solitaire. Edward Abbey. Tucson: University of Arizona Press, 2010.

The Monkey Wrench Gang. Edward Abbey. New York: HarperCollins, 2014.

ENVIRONMENTAL ORGANIZATIONS

Southern Utah Wilderness Alliance
https://suwa.org

Grand Canyon Trust
https://www.grandcanyontrust.org

The Bears Ears Inter-Tribal Coalition
http://bearsearscoalition.org

The Sierra Club
https://www.sierraclub.org

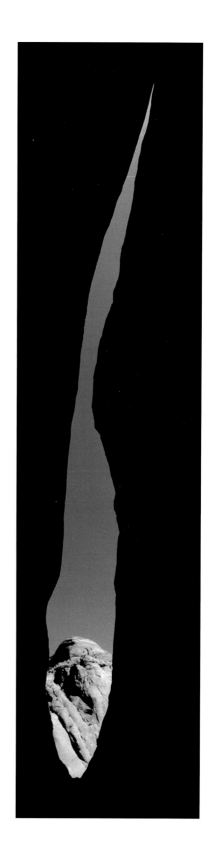

RMB | Rocky Mountain Books Ltd.
rmbooks.com
@rmbooks
facebook.com/rmbooks

Cataloguing data available from Library and Archives Canada
ISBN 9781771602587 (hardcover)

Printed and bound in Canada by Friesens

Distributed in Canada by Heritage Group Distribution and in the U.S. by Publishers Group West

For information on purchasing bulk quantities of this book, or to obtain media excerpts or invite the author to speak at an event, please visit rmbooks.com and select the "Contact Us" tab.

We acknowledge the financial support of the Government of Canada through the Canada Book Fund and the Canada Council for the Arts, and of the province of British Columbia through the British Columbia Arts Council and the Book Publishing Tax Credit.

Trying for a better vantage point: You can't make long exposures when swinging from a rope. Our invented "slotpod," with its adjustable wooden legs, proved to be a finicky, only slightly better camera mount.